CW00501346

The Honest Handbooks

The Simple Rules of Project Management

Proven and practical rules
to become a successful
project manager

Victor SIXTIN

Copyright

The Simple Rules of Project Management

Also in *The Honest Handbooks* series

The Simple Rules of Getting A Lot Done,
Victor Sixtin

About *The Honest Handbooks*

The Honest Handbooks are a series of useful books for professionals. They are books that get straight to the point, with clear, actionable recommendations based on years of experience in trenches.

In a nutshell: what you should know when taking on a new job.

There are thousands of clever management/business/leadership/self-development books written by smart people. They develop and present around three to six main ideas and spread them out over hundreds of pages.

After hours of reading, you hopefully get the big picture, but you have no clue where to start if you want to implement part or all of it.

The *Honest Handbooks* are the exact opposite: short, easy-to-read books with clear step-by-step actions to take right away. Every book can be read in two hours or less. They are based on practical rules with short, detailed instructions for implementation.

Once you've read each rule's section, take a moment to reflect and imagine how you could put it into practice. The information is accessible and designed to encourage the reader to refer back to it often and read it over and over again.

The *Honest Handbooks* are not written by journalists or scholars. We love you guys; you have great views and interesting insights, but real corporate life cannot be learned in books and through studies.

Preface to *The Simple Rules of Project Management*

I'm not a start-up guru nor a TED Talk speaker. I don't wake up at 5 a.m. to run 10k on the beach before meditating. I'm a regular corporate guy, not here to change your life with revolutionary concepts, but simply to try to help with good advice that comes from practical experience.

You won't find me on linked-in. I maintain anonymity as I am still actively employed in the field. I want to protect my position at my current employer, along with my freedom to be able to write what I want.

Here's my background.

Trained in engineering, I started as a consultant in business strategy and transformation, supporting various companies on digital, client, and distribution matters. This experience sharpened my ability to deliver exceptional work, take charge of expansive projects, and lead sizable teams effectively.

A big international retailer asked me then to help plan its digital transformation and helm a series of major innovation projects. Working with this $100 billion company, I developed a nuanced understanding of corporate dynamics and the art of steering through the complex governance of large organizations.

Most recently, I've served as the head of digital and innovation at a worldwide product company. Our work in designing, building, and selling products has been met with tremendous success, generating tens of billions in revenue and sustaining a healthy profit margin. In this conservative, because very successful, company, I've mastered the nuances of being a persuasive change agent, driving innovation and progress.

In my personal life, I'm a happy husband and father of two daughters. I love to have a great work-life balance to have time for my friends and family and sports.

This book is a distillation of my experiences, a testament to the power of *Project Management* and how it changes the world.

The simple rules of project management

The Honest Handbooks

Introduction

I love project management.

For the project manager, every year is different, every week is different, and every day he
learns something. There's no "typical day."
At the end of the road, there's a result:
something that was not here before, a product that's going to be useful to someone, an
achievement to be proud of.

It's been almost 20 years since my first
project. I've had the opportunity to manage
many, some small, some big, in all kinds of
organizations and with different types of
stakeholders. I remember every one of them:
the team, the stakes, the challenges, the hard
times, the good times.

The Simple Rules of Project Management

Now, being a manager of project managers, I want to pass on and share what I've learned along the way.

Being a project manager is rewarding but difficult, often stressful, and sometimes unfair.

The question you may be wondering is: did the world really need a new book about project management? There are already lots of books out there (over 50,000 on Amazon).

Most of them are good and valuable, but most of them teach theory.
If you want to be a project manager, you must read them. Mastering the core hard skills of project management is mandatory. You can't manage a project if you don't know what a Gantt chart is, what risks are, what the word governance means, etc.

There are different frameworks. I am a Project Management Institute disciple; the PM-

Bok is my bible.

These books describe what a perfect project looks like. They lack the taste of a real project when you are on the front line, responsible for high stakes, and dealing with real people who have their own concerns and priorities.

As a junior project manager, I was fortunate enough to be supported by experienced managers who guided me through the different steps of my first project. They did tell me what was not told in books.

Leading junior project managers today, I try in my turn to guide and teach them how to lead a project and operate through the intricacies of a real organization.

This book is a collection of the advice I give along the way.
In practice, they're spread over months. Here, they're packed in one small book.

There are 48 rules.

Some are unexpected, others seem obvious. Some are long; others are short. But they are equally important. Failing one of them will hurt your project.

They are roughly organized according to the classic chronology of a project, although some rules apply to the whole project.

On your first read, I would recommend going through the book from start to finish. Then, you'll be able to come back to the right rule whenever you need to, depending on the situation you face in your project.

1

A project delivers something new

It's important to identify what a project is from what it isn't—a project versus daily operations—because they require opposite management practices.

A project delivers something that has never been done before. It has a start, and it has an end. It draws on finite resources.

If what you have to do:

-   Has already been done and needs to

be repeated
- Improves or maintains an existing product
- Delivering a product continuously without an end

That is day-to-day business life. It's not a project. Stakes, challenges, and management skills are different. You can stop reading this book.

Lots of people are managing a department or a domain, doing more or less the same thing over and over again. They may call themselves project managers, but they aren't.

A project is:
- doing (building or coding) something totally new,
- in a limited timeframe,
- with limited resources.

A project is a jump into the unknown. It's something nobody has done before; otherwise, it's not a project.

It is an epic journey where you'll be the main character, hopefully the hero. There will be allies and oppositions. Trials will have to be faced. You'll have to deal with uncertainty. Face change and embrace it. It's exhilarating.

Like any adventure, the more prepared you are, the better. The fundamentals of Project Management are your tools, so know your basics: what's a planning, a budget, a governance…

Be ready to explore, discover, and face the unexpected.
Later, a project often turns into a story, sometimes a legend, you will be eager to share.

2

Before you start, scope

There's work to do before starting the project.

You wouldn't build a house without the blueprints and a price, would you? Well, your management won't allow you to start a project without a detailed planning and a budget.

This phase is called the *scoping*.

It's my favorite part of a project, which is funny because it's before the project.

A blank page (or slide) is facing you. Everything is new; everything is possible.

Usually, you will inherit a pretty short request from someone like: "We'd like to tackle this challenge." It's what I call a "post-it requirement." It is vague and not detailed. The fun thing is that, in many cases, it isn't clearer in anyone else's head, even from the people who expressed the idea in the first place.

There's usually an unclear perception of the concern, the pain point to heal, but that's it. Nobody knows exactly what should be done.

The first thing to do is to get clarity. There are three main parts to expound:
- The need (the why): what is the problem to be solved?
- The solution (the what): what is the right solution?
- The approach (the how): what does it

take to build the solution?

Basically, you set the stage and propose an objective and a series of actions that come with it. You say what you need (i.e., how much money and how much time).

But how do you do that? Chances are you don't know anything about the matter or the potential solutions.

You turn into a detective.

Take your pencil and notebook, and go talk to people.

Start with the people expressing the need. Meet them, chat with them, and live a day of their life to understand the problem to solve. Eventually, they might have a small idea of what the solution could look like.

Investigate. Meet all the people you can, from the people who could have an idea of what could be good solutions to the problem to the ones who can tell you what it would take to build the solution.

The more people you meet, the better. The key word in this first phase is curiosity.

Each project will require a specific approach: different problems, different people to meet, different solutions, and different approaches. But the scoping phase deliverable always has the same structure and develops the same chapters, widely covered in the traditional project management books:

- Context: why are we talking about this? Why now?
- Purpose: what do we propose to build to answer what challenge?
- Goals: what are the tangible benefits expected from the project?
- Scope: what exactly will be delivered?
- Out of scope: what is not going to be delivered? Why?
- Approach: what are activities that are

going to be performed?

- Planning: when those tasks are scheduled? How are they tiled and/or dependent?
- Team: who is going to be drafted on the project?
- Budget: how much is it going to cost?
- Return on investment: how much the company will gain/save thanks to the project?
- Risks: what event could alter the course of the project? What do we suggest to control their impact?
- Governance: how are we going to monitor and steer the project?

Remember, at this phase of the project, everything can be changed. Once the scoping is finished and the project is started, it will be much more difficult to change things (goals, timing, or budget).

The deliverable is a comprehensive deck that will be your bible for the project. Every time you meet or onboard someone new, you'll be able to easily present why he's contacted and what is expected from him.

At the end of the phase, you will present this scoping to the top management for them to decide whether to launch the project.
Launching the project means giving you the resources (money, people, etc.) you asked for.

It's like a contract you sign with your company. If they give you what you asked for, you must deliver what you presented.

Be diligent in your scoping phase; don't cut corners.

3

Scope the scoping

Fun fact: some scoping might be so heavy that it can be approached as a project that needs to be scoped.

Of course, the idea is not to enter an endless loop. You won't have to scope the scoping of the scoping phase. No.

But during the scoping of the project, you will solicit a lot of people. As a reminder, as a project manager, you cannot be an expert in the relevant subjects. You'll need to meet with the end users to understand their needs and pain points. You'll need to meet with the people who can build the solution that will resolve the challenge so they can explain to you what needs to be done.

Maybe those people will have some home-work, like estimating how much time and money a specific task can take. In the end, contributing to a scoping phase can repre-sent hours or days of work for people who already have their usual days to deliver. Multiply that by the sum of people you need to interview, and you can quickly reach fig-ures in the dozens, sometimes hundreds of man-days, meaning a lot of money.

Try to identify the key people you would have to meet and how much time you'll need.

Put that down on paper: what you're about to do and the people you will need help from.

Hence, you'll be able to get the validation from the management to start your scoping phase and to request some other people's time.

Don't worry, it's a couple of hours work. Just 2 to 3 slides, with a quick intro, who you think you need to see, and the time frame. It will pave the way to a smooth and great scoping.

4

Write meeting minutes

Minutes are so 20th century. We are in a fast-paced world now, and agile methods have been widely adopted. What's the point of losing time writing down what we discussed? We trust each other, right? Let's focus on delivery rather than administrative tasks.

You couldn't be more wrong.

Writing minutes saves time.
Meeting minutes will save you time throughout your entire project. So, I advise you to start as early as possible.

You'll lose time at the start of every meeting if you don't have previous meeting minutes. You will lose time after the meetings when you'll try to remember what has been said and what has been decided. You will lose time replaying the meeting with everyone if you don't have the same recollection of it.

Choose your favorite channel: e-mail, Word, Excel, or PowerPoint.

Maximum 36 hours after every meeting, there must be an e-mail (and probably an attached document) presenting who was there, what has been discussed, what are the decisions taken, and what are the next steps.

They are the only way to track delivery in your team. If you're waiting for someone to do something, how can you pressure him if you don't have anything written to expose?

Minutes enable the project to be under

healthy pressure. The more impactful and regular they are, the more reactive your team will be. If you're lazy with your minutes, don't expect your team to be diligent in their tasks.

5

Identify sponsor(s)

A sponsor is a top manager who will be accountable for the project's success or failure.

He/they will be your main support of the project, maybe your lifeline if things go rough.

His (or her) role is important.

If everything is going well, his main role is to be the face of the project at whatever grade level he is.

If things get complicated, his support could be critical if tough decisions have to be made.

Regardless of the circumstances, the higher its position within the company, the better. But be careful not to aim too high. If the sponsor is out of your league, there is little chance he will find an interest in the project, and he won't be involved in the project.

There could be several sponsors depending on who will use/build the product. That's ok.

Identifying the sponsor starts at the very beginning of the project. As the project manager, you must identify who could take on the role. In most of the projects, the sponsor is quite obvious; it's a top executive above the team expressing the need, who often is the guy engaging the budget of the project.

Meet him and formally ask him to endorse the project and, if he agrees, to take the role of sponsor.

It's a commitment you should not take lightly, as its presence will be mandatory in several committees.

An absent sponsor is useless.

6

Start with the problem,
not the solution

Too many projects start with a solution in mind:

"We need to have that famous software."

"Let's build this thing we saw in a fair or magazine."

This is the best and fastest way to end up with something that works but that nobody will use because it doesn't meet any needs.

Of course, having potential solutions in mind

can be useful to trigger conversations during the scoping phase. But the why of the project must be carefully assessed.

Talk to the end users. Not the end users' manager, the real end user. Spend time with them. Watch them working, ask them to show you what's not working, and let them tell you what their dream day could look like tomorrow. You need to delve deep into the subjects.

Once you understand the problem, thanks to a deep empathy, you can start to explore serious, potential solutions.

7

Choose good goals

Goals are what will validate whether you did a good job (or not).

Lots of books have been written about goals. Google "SMART goals" (Specific, Measurable, Achievable, Relevant, Time-bound); it's a great start.

A goal cannot be "build this in 8 months."

Anyone can do something totally useless in a couple of months.

A goal must be business-oriented. Are you

43

going to improve sales? Improve margins? Improve efficiency? Cut costs? Whatever it is, identify your impact.

A goal must be quantified. You must be able to say how much money the company will save or gain per year. Everything can be evaluated.

Do not settle for vague, not specific goals.

How I translate SMART:

- Specific: simple, complex goals are smoke and mirrors
- Measurable: have a unit
- Achievable: realistic, don't try to solve world hunger
- Relevant: make sense for the company
- Time-bound: have an end date. Unless you're working on nuclear plants or in the space industry, aim for less than 5 years away.

You must know what you're bringing to

your company, what you're chasing, and how what you're building is going to help. When you have mediation to make during the project because of issues or surprises, you'll have to be able to measure the impact a change of plan will have on your goals.

The good news is you write your goals. You're judge and executioner. It's up to you to choose realistic goals, so you have a great chance to reach them but are ambitious enough for the project to be interesting.

The bad news is that you'll have no excuse if you fail.

Let's be honest: in the end, chances are no one will confront you with the goals you presented at the beginning of the project.

Nonetheless, as a project manager, you should take great care in defining your goals because poorly defined goals are hardly reachable or valuable.

8

Break down the work, from top to bottom

Big tasks cannot be properly assessed. Small ones can.

The more you chop down your project into smaller chunks, the more you'll be able to build an accurate plan, and the easier it will be to manage the project later.

A project manager must think top-down, breaking down the global project into different parts or workstreams, each one of them broken down into smaller streams, and so on.

When you can't break down anymore, then you can begin to plan.
Don't try to plan a project from the bottom up; it is the best way to forget an entire part of it.

Let's take an example: your birthday party.

The first level of deconstruction could be:
- The guests
- The invitations
- The place
- The music
- The food and drinks

Then, if you break down the *place* stream, you have the following sub-streams:
- The location
- Tables and chairs
- Amenities
- Transportation
- Cleaning

- Decoration

Then, you break down these sub-streams and so on until you can't no more.

It's the best and easiest way to have a holistic approach to the project. Each workstream and sub-workstream can be assessed and often managed independently, even though they could be interdependencies.

Once you have reached the right level of deconstruction, identifying the action to take will be easy. I like to break down my tasks into actions that take a few days, a maximum of one week. At this level, having a good understanding of the action and its owner is easier for the project manager.

During the project, this logical organization will ease the progress and budget monitoring and help you give clear reporting.

9

Planning is like story-boarding

Now that the project has been broken down, it's time to set all these tasks in motion and write the story that will lead to the product delivery.

The more precise, the better.

Beyond the task itself, it is very important to identify all the actors that will have a role to play and how much time they will need.

There's an interesting parallel to make with

the movie industry.

During the preparation of a movie, the director prepares a storyboard. It's a succession of drawings presenting each scene: where it takes place, what's the set, who's acting, what are the costumes, what are the shooting angles…

When the movie hits the theaters, it's impressive how close it is to the storyboard. Often, you're wondering if the drawings were done after the movie. The storyboard is the embodiment of how the director imagines the movie.

The process of planification should be very close to that. The planning must be the embodiment of how the project manager sees the project to come. At the end of the project, someone studying the initial planning should be amazed by how close it described how the project would unfold.

For the project manager in the scoping phase,

visualizing how each task would take place is a powerful tool. It helps to ensure that the project manager has a good understanding of what they need to perform, and it helps secure the sequence of tasks.

It will also help to identify that every input required will be ready and available when the task is expected to begin.

10

Know your stuff, don't be fooled

It's not mandatory to be experienced in a field to be a good project manager. But it helps.

There are two main traps for the non-expert project manager.

During the scoping of the project, some actors might try to overestimate tasks. They could try to add some time-buffer. They could request more resources than needed. They would do that to limit stress on their side or to compensate for the pressure they could have with other projects that have challenged them. You could understand or accept that. The problem is that if everyone does that on all the tasks, the project will take 20% more time and or money to be completed.

After the project kick-off, people could try to hide or minimize the challenges they could face. They would be fuzzy about where they are, assuring everything is under control. Sometimes, they manage to put the work back on track. Often, they finish to open and share their trouble, but it's too late; the only thing you can do is acknowledge the delay and reschedule the following tasks.

The only way to avoid those situations is to be able to challenge your interlocutors.

But how can you do that when you don't know much? By being deeply curious, genuinely deeply curious. "Explain it to me like I'm 5 years old" should be your favorite line.

From the very beginning, spend time with everyone, live their daily routine, and experience their pain points. Try to see to understand. During the scoping phase, it's "show me something similar you're working on so I can understand what you'll do during the project."

During the project, it's "show me what you're doing so I can understand where you are and where you're heading."

By being absolutely interested, you'll be a quick learner, and you won't be easily misled.

11

Provision some buffer

Now that you have collected all the tasks of your project, there's a last thing you must carefully design: your buffer.

A buffer is a little envelope you have for any surprise. There should be a time buffer and a money buffer.

The idea is that a task taking slightly more or longer than expected does not necessarily lead to a delay at the end of a project. Same for the budget.

There's a trick. On the one hand, you're expected to have a buffer. On the other, you'll be challenged on the length and budget of every task. Hiding a buffer in a project plan is a subtle art.

Plus, people tend to take all the time they're given to deliver. If a team evaluated a task to be 2 weeks long, if you say it will take 3 weeks, there's a chance the team will lower the pressure and take, let's say, 2 weeks and a half to do it. It's not what you want, either.

You must be creative. I include tasks for reviewing deliverables or preparing for committee meetings or important deadlines, which I can compress if necessary.

A 5% to 10% buffer on both budget and timeline is a good rough estimate.

During the project, the buffer will live. Some tasks will take less than expected, others more. Don't share it.

This is your little secret.

12

Build a business plan, even if not required

Rentability is an easy concept to understand: how much you will gain versus how much it costs. You might expect most of the companies to be driven by the Return On Interest of any initiative they engage.

Yet, in most companies I worked for, I've observed a relative lack of thoroughness regarding the analysis of the return on investment of the projects to be engaged.

Costs are generally mandatory. And even the

costs are often required on a limited scope: only external costs, suppliers/contractors, or direct costs.

For the benefits, projects will often be flagged as "strategic" or "brand development" or anything justifying that it's too complicated to estimate any number.

It is, therefore, likely that you won't be overly challenged on the ROI of your project or even that you won't be asked anything at all.

However, I would highly recommend you spend some serious time on the topic.

Estimating the rentability of your project requires you to anticipate precisely what your project will earn or save and to identify how much it will cost to build and maintain.

Start with the costs; it's the easy part. There are all the direct costs: the raw materials, the machines, the real estate, etc. Every minute spent by anyone in the company on the project shall also be seen as a cost, no matter the purpose (delivery, design, management, HR, etc.). Finally, you must evaluate all the costs necessary for the operational maintenance of your product.

On the benefits side, there's first the direct profits like new sales, rise in existing sales, or manufacturing cost optimization. Then, you have more indirect gains: direct administrative tasks, accelerations, retail productivity optimization, and so on.

All those lines must be carefully estimated. It's not always easy; people may disagree, but it's mandatory. You cannot settle for: "average customer loyalty will increase." How much will it increase? With an average frequency and basket, you can deduct the increase.

Each line must end with $, not %.

The Simple Rules of Project Management

Do the exercise over a 5-year period unless otherwise instructed in your company.

As a project manager, you should care about how your work will influence the company. You must have a very detailed understanding of all the impacts of the project.

Long-term speaking, it's important for your career to be sure you're bringing value to your company (and eventually to the world).

In the short term, many advantages. First, it helps you ensure you master the totality of the ends and means of your project. Then, when you have trade-offs to take, and you'll have, you will be able to quickly assess their impacts on the figures you sold at the beginning of the project.

13

If you're the pig, don't start

Do you know the story of the pig and the chicken?

It's about commitment.

From *Wikipedia*:

> A Pig and a Chicken are walking down the road.
> The Chicken says, "Hey Pig, I was thinking we should open a restaurant!"

Pig replies, "Hm, maybe; what would we call it?"

The Chicken responds, "How about Ham-n-Eggs?"

The Pig thinks for a moment and says, "No thanks. I'd be committed, but you'd only be involved."

In many projects, the level of commitment of the different stakeholders is not the same.

Some will be 100% committed; they will have their careers at stake. If the project fails, at best, it's a stop in their evolution; at worst, they are fired.

Others will be involved. They'll be around while everything goes well. But at first sight of trouble, they will take their distance. If the project fails, it will not be their responsibility. "I did not choose the solution," "They did not understand my requirements," or "I didn't have a say in the matter" are things you might hear.

At this point, you'll have to fully endorse the responsibility for the failure, even if the other side has his share of responsibility.

This is not extreme; it happens, especially in big projects and in big companies.

Everyone's full commitment is mandatory to ensure a smooth and good project execution.

It will lead to thorough phases of requirements gathering, design, testing, and change management. It will help make an easy launch.

Involve every key stakeholder from the scoping and then at each step and decision of the project. Ask them their opinion and what they recommend. Every time, write meeting minutes and share them. During committees, include them in the presentation of recommendations and deliverables.

Don't request their signature at the end of every phase, but nearly.

14

The governance set the pace

Governance on paper is not complicated. You'll find in any management book that you'll need a project committee with the core team and a steering committee with the sponsors.

In practice, envisioning the right entities with the right cast is a delicate exercise.

The governance gives the pace and intensity of the project. Choose a bi-monthly executive steering committee, which is unusually often, and you'll be sure that people in the company will prioritize you. Choose a quarterly executive steering committee, which is unusually distant, and it will be hard to get things done in between.

Hence, you might be tempted to schedule often. But if you don't have anything, progress or decisions, to present to the committee, you won't have a warm welcome. And sponsors won't show up after your second useless committee.

There are three dimensions to play with:

- The type of committees to organize (steering committee (executive or not), project committee, topic-specific committee): it must be clear what every instance's purpose is.
- The invitees: the team, their boss, their boss's boss, the contractors. Be sure that at every meeting, there are the right people to present and the right people to take the awaited de-

cision.

- The frequency: weekly, bi-monthly, monthly, quarterly. It gives a sense of urgency to the project.

During the scoping of the project, draft different propositions and share them with the key stakeholders to get their thoughts. Take the feedback, iterate, and present the different layers of committees, their role, and level of decision in your scoping document. Present the governance when you engage the project to formally approve it.

In the hours after the project kick-off, schedule all the committees for the next 12 months, even if you need to move them later.

15

You don't choose
your team

The quality of the team is the most critical
success factor of a project.

The bad news is you won't choose your
team.

During the scoping of the project, the project
manager navigates the organization, wondering what needs to be built, how it can be
built, and who could build it.

In the departments you have identified as
having a role in the project, you will meet

the manager and ask who the best people for the jobs to be done are. The trick is that the "best" is often replaced by "available." Chances are the department manager won't ask you who you'd like to work with, even with the available resources. He will designate who will take part in the project.

The small, good news is there's an exception to the rule.

If contractors are needed, the project manager has a role and voice in the selection process. In that case, it's important to be specific in the request for proposal on the kind of profiles that are expected. Be demanding of the consultants and partners who might join the project, as they could play an important role in the unfolding of the story.

In the end, you might end up with a bunch of opposite people with different cultures, ages, and personalities. They might not look like the best fit. But it's the role of the project manager to draw the best out of the team. The great project manager knows how to create an alchemy from ingredients that may not be compatible, just like any sports coach does with his teams.

16

There's not enough room for two project managers

One could divide a project team into two main parts.

There are those who say what they want and will test the product to validate it and then use it.

And there are those who build the product.

In lots of companies, both sides want to have their pilot. The project ends up with two managers. And when two people are in charge, things get complicated.

One project manager means one person is accountable for planning, reporting, and animation. When someone has a question, a request, or a claim, she knows who to contact.

When there are two project managers, it's not clear who oversees what, who reports what to whom, and so on. It needs additional coordination, and it may lead to loopholes.

This question of one vs several project managers is often deeply rooted in an organization's culture and habits.

If someone has been named to lead the project with you, it won't be easy to recommend naming only one project manager.

What you do is work on the RACI.

The RACI is the table listing all the tasks of the project, including management ones, and explicitly says who is Responsible (meaning the one who performs the task), who is Accountable, who is Consulted, and who is Involved.

If you want to have a drive and control of the project, I recommend that you focus on management tasks, not representation.

Leave some decision-making and steering committee preparation responsibilities to your counterpart. Take on what seems to be boring tasks: planning, budgeting, governance, workshop planning, attendance, and so on. Thus, you'll have an operational view of the project, understanding what's going on, the difficulties, and the challenges. You'll be on the critical path, and you'll be able to steer the project on all layers.

In the end, you will see that you will still have a key role in representing the project because you alone will understand its ins and outs.

17

Powerpoint is a project manager's best friend

There are a lot of fancy project management tools, the most famous being Microsoft Project and Excel, to a certain extent.

Among other things, they allow you to build Gantt charts with links between tasks. For big projects with hundreds of tasks, they are mandatory. It's the only way to see how a small change can impact the other downstream and to manage the workload of a big team over time.

But even in those big projects, that kind of

tool is not used by the project manager. In such cases needing advanced features, the project manager is supported by a Project Management Office (PMO). It's a team (sometimes a team of one) handling all administrative tasks such as activity reporting, progress monitoring, project reporting, committee scheduling, and so on. The PMO is the power user of project management tools, not the project manager.

What you will really need is a tool that helps him convey messages. A project manager's job is to tell stories, explain what has been done, and explain what comes next. And there's no better tool for that than Microsoft PowerPoint (Apple Keynote, if you think differently).

You can put every message on a slide: a project context and goals, a macro planning and the actualized one, a global budget and the adjusted one, a risk and different mitigation scenarios.

Furthermore, PowerPoint is very flexible. It's easy to pick slides from past presentations, prepare new ones, and adapt slides to fit the messages.

The project manager will spend a great deal of his time on PowerPoint, either preparing or presenting decks. So, you better be skilled in PowerPoint.

18

Engage the project

Most of the things we've seen before were not part of the project. They were part of the scoping.

You've put together a great scoping document. The problem to tackle has been carefully phrased, and you know exactly what and who it would take to build the right solution.

Every key stakeholder has reviewed and validated the document and is fully involved in the initiative.

It's time to offer the project to the company

management to get the official seal of approval.

In some companies, those engagement ceremonies are a regular commission with permanent members, more or less the same as the executive committee.

If there's no such authority in your organization, it's the right moment to convene your steering committee for the first time.

It's very easy to prepare because you will present an executive summary of your scoping document.

To put it simply, you say: "If you give me this money, I will deliver this in X months."

Be careful; what you present is bonding. If they give you what you ask and you miss your target, it will be on you.
Of course, whatever the decision, write the meeting minutes and share it with everyone.

19

Kick-off

Once the leadership has formally approved your project, you must make it official and put everyone in motion.

Gather every key player of the project in a room, with their manager if possible. Of course, you will have sent the meeting request before the engagement meeting to have the maximum number of people present.

The sponsor's presence is mandatory. He usually introduces the meeting with a small motivational speech, reaffirming the stakes and goals of the project.

The rest of the content of the meeting is basically the same as the engagement meeting, except that you should share the floor. Invite key stakeholders to present some part of the project.

The most important is the presentation of the planning. You might want to present a planning a little bit more detailed than during the engagement meeting. Outline the most important milestones and try to set some symbolic deadlines in everyone's head.

Besides, there must be a focus on the coming 6 to 8 weeks with the list of all the tasks that have to be started.

Introduce the team; everyone must be able to identify who will do what.
Detail the governance and the coming committees with their approximate date. Tell them that the meeting requests have already been sent or that they are coming soon.

Right after the kick-off, the meeting requests for all the workshops and key meetings of the first 2 months must be sent.

Meetings with the individuals who are to start the initial tasks should also be scheduled for the following day.

20

Rituals bind the team together

When everyone's working alone, delivering their task on their own without communicating with others, you don't have a team. At the first sign of misalignment, at the first mistake, it will explode. A cohesive team is key to going through all the project turbulences in complete serenity.

Weekly committees do not build a team; you must do more than that.

The key players, your core team, must meet

regularly and informally. Breakfast, coffee, lunch, beer after work, etc., you must find what fits most with the individualities and their constraints.

Those privileged moments together should happen at least twice a month.

Do not hesitate to iterate if you feel the selected approach does not work. Each team is unique, and things that may have worked in a previous project with different people might not work on this one.

Moreover, as the project manager, you must physically meet every member of the core team alone at least once every two days, even if just 30 minutes.

I also recommend meeting every member of the project at least once a month.

During intense periods, like the start of the project, the beginning of the tests, or the prelaunch weeks, daily standup meetings are a good way to keep a close-knit team and a good dynamic.

All those little things should start right from the beginning of the project.

21

Connect with the sponsor

A direct and continuous bond between the sponsor and the project manager is to be built during the scoping and reinforced during the project.

The sponsor holds a high position within the organization.

By carefully and regularly reporting the progress of the project, he will be a great advisor. He will be able to tell you things that happen elsewhere in the company that could impact your project. He will also identify the blind spots you might have and identify people you must care about.

Things you will discuss won't be on the steering committee's agenda.

Chances are he's a successful professional that will help you grow personally. The project is an opportunity for you to catch up with him often and to learn a lot.

He's also here to support the project during hard times. But you can't reach out to him after weeks of silence when there's fire all over the place. You must provide diligent reporting and share any difficulties you're facing from the very start.

Right after the engagement meeting, schedule a monthly informal one-to-one with your sponsor for the duration of the project.

22

Organize knowledge management

A small project generates megabytes of data every week. For medium to large projects, you can expect hundreds of documents and versions every week.

If you don't organize how deliverables must be named and classified, you and your team will lose lots of precious time.

Don't think you can manage it only with the help of a search engine, or you're going to be disappointed.

Only three elements enable you to have well-organized stuff:

- A platform: Google Docs, Share-Point, teams, confluence, shared folder... They all have their pros and cons. The choice is yours; there should be a preferred option in your company. The only thing you have to do is to create your project in the tool and make sure all the team can access it.
- A hierarchy: The easiest way is to go for the project planning streams and sub-streams. Initiate the folders and subfolders when you create the project in the platform.
- A file naming system: This one is more for big projects because more difficult to implement but very powerful. Example:
- ProjectName_Workstream_Deliverable_Version_Author.Extension

Try to gather templates or past deliverables from previous projects to initiate example folders for the main tasks.

Ideally, this knowledge management system is part of your scoping document and a small part of your kick-off meeting.

It deserves a dedicated e-mail in the first days of the project. The more you wait, the more complicated it will be to enforce the rules and recover the past files.

23

Post clear progress updates

The easier it is for anyone to understand the status of your project, the more you will be appreciated.

Surprisingly, the number of black box projects is incredible. It's impossible to understand what their planning is and to get a clear understanding of their progress.

Hope you don't have to coordinate with such a project. Because you would have to lose lots of time desperately looking for a deck of a not-so-long-ago committee and hope there's something as close as possible to up-dated planning. And you'll curse the project manager as much as you can. No need to say such project managers have a bad reputation.

It doesn't take much to provide visibility on your project:

- an actualized macro-planning (a planning that fits in 1 slide) with a big red "we are here" label and
- a sum-up of last month's and next month's activities.

Every month, you send this to the team, the company's management, and every person who has shown any interest in the project at some point.

Here again, you will save time. Every time you meet someone external from the project, it will be very easy to show where you are and eventually where you need them.

Quickly, you'll see that the more reporting you give, the fewer questions people will ask.

24

Master the triangle scope - cost – planning

The famous triangle scope-budget–planning looks like an abstract concept, perfect for books and management schools.

But it's very real, you'll experience it very quickly.

A quick reminder of the triangle: what you do, how much it costs, and how long it will take are strongly linked.

Change one, and you'll impact at least one other.

If you have more resources (people or money), you can do the same thing quicker, or you can do more in the same planning. If you want to save money, you can do less.

If you extend the schedule, you'll be able to accomplish more (but it will often cost you more).

If you want to do more, you'll need more time and money.

A project manager's goal is not to lock the triangle. On the opposite, he must master it in order to manage it with fluidity.

On a daily basis, you will need to reallocate time or resources between tasks or adjust the expected outcome up or down.

A lot can happen during the project. At some point, you might be way above the expected budget or behind schedule. The buffers added here and there to absorb the delays may not be sufficient. In that case, different scenarios will have to be designed for the Steering Committee. Usually, two options are presented:

- From that point, the initial planning can still be respected, but it will cost more, or the initial scope won't be delivered.
- It will cost more (and often take longer).

More occasionally, but still relatively likely, you may be asked by your management to reduce your budget. You should welcome such requests with ease and immediately bounce back by asking which part of the deliverable needs to be removed, while promptly suggesting a few proposals. This way you will show that you are a facilitator and that you have a good grasp of your project.

25

Own your scope

The scope of a project is vulnerable; it requires safeguarding throughout the project.

During the scoping of your project, you have defined its scope. You said what you were going to do. You said what you were not going to do.

Strangely, people tend to forget what was said, validated, and engaged.
During the project, they will try to load your boat.

There could be many reasons for those

change requests, the most common being an omission in the requirements.

That's not acceptable because a change in scope implies a change in the budget and the planning.

From the very start of the project, you must be very clear on what your scope is. You must repeat you're scope as much as possible. At every steering committee, there must be a slide where you recall in detail what you're going to do.

Of course, if the steering committee asks for the scope to be amended, you can't say no. As you've been very clear that it was not in your initial scope, no one will be surprised when you say that you need to assess the impact of that change on the budget and the planning.

You present the scenarios, and you act on the decision: change or don't change the scope, the planning, and the budget.

When the change request is validated, you have a new scope.

What do you do with your new scope? You represent it in the next steering committee.

26

Master your landing

The budget must be monitored at the finest possible granularity.

At any point, you must have a very accurate view of what you've spent. At least every month, everyone should provide you with how much time or money they've spent at the task level.

Of course, to be useful, you must know how much this person was supposed to spend.

Then, you must update what was planned for the tasks in progress and the following ones. Maybe things might be tougher than expected, and other tasks might be revised upward. Maybe some difficulties have been tackled in a task that cost more than expected, but it should facilitate downstream work so you can revise some other tasks.

Thus, you'll have an updated landing plan and a new estimate of the global budget you need.

At every steering committee, you must present your budget status in the same way you present a planning update.

Small budget variations can happen. It's ok. Big changes can also happen if there's a change in the scope. But unforeseen, unexplained budget increases are unforgivable.

Be careful; numbers are easier to analyze than the quality of your delivery. Even if you meet initial requirements, overspending the budget is frowned upon unless carefully and dutifully explained.

27

The coffee machine is your second office

A project is won at the coffee machine.

The main added value of the project manager is not micromanaging the team. His role is to navigate the project through all the different hazards that may arise.

You can't do that behind your computer or in a meeting room. Because when the information hits you through the mail or in a meeting, it's too late. The fact is established. You can only react.

A project manager must collect clues. It takes human connection and emotional engagement. That's the only way to have a true and deep conversation where you're going to get valuable information.

There's no better place to do that than the coffee machine (well, there's the smoking area, but I won't promote smoking as a key skill of a project manager).

It can also be through casual lunch or drink outside the building. But the coffee machine has this priceless serendipity, those unexpected encounters that can change everything.

From one conversation to another, you will collect dots. By connecting those dots between them, you'll be able to identify risks and opportunities for your project and take action.

28

Open to your peers

In every company, in every department, there's a kind of competition, sometimes quiet, sometimes sharp, between people of similar positions.

Each person tends to withdraw into themselves, afraid of sharing their secret sauce or losing some scope to others.

It's surprising as it's rapidly evident that most open and extroverted individuals are more successful than their counterparts. They reach out to others, looking for advice or any thought that could help them.

They talk simply with their boss. They share what they have on their mind when meeting someone.

You will be surprised by the number of people who have had similar past experiences to the one you are encountering.

Obviously, it will not capsize what you do and how you do it.

From simple conversations, you will catch small chunks of ideas that will slightly enhance what you do. By doing it every day of every week, you will keep on adding those small improvements with an exponential effect.

And even if they can't help you, the process of articulating what you have on your mind is already extremely helpful.

29

Be transparent,
be stressless

Being a project manager should be the easi-est job on earth.

You don't deliver anything; hence, if some-thing goes wrong, it cannot be your fault. Whatever happens, you cannot be blamed.

Yet, a lot of project managers carry immense stress on their shoulders.

It's because they lack transparency.

It comes from good intentions; they try to protect the team.

A team member did a poor job estimating the time and resources needed for a task, and now the project is behind schedule or above budget. Another project has been running late, a key resource has not been released as soon as expected, and now the project is behind schedule.

You don't want to blame the team; it's already tough for them. Maybe you'll be able to catch up later. You take on you, and you don't share those difficulties for now.

Here comes the stress.

Shit happens, everyone can understand that, even your boss.

Everyone is doing their best. If there's been an error during the scoping phase, so be it. Maybe they lacked some information at the time. If a task takes longer than expected, there may be good reason.

The worst thing a project manager can do is withhold information. Hiding difficulties from the steering committee, hoping a situation will improve by itself.

An unexpected delay should be detected quickly, before the middle of the awaited duration. At this moment, your role as a project manager is to spot the trend and check with the team member if he can catch up, how he will do it, what he would eventually need to do so, or if it's going to end with several weeks of delay.

The project manager then shares the situation during the next steering committee. You will present the whole situation and offer mitigation plans (reinforce the team, reorganize tasks, alter planning, etc.).
Whatever the committee decides, your job is done.

The diligent and transparent project manager has no stress because the steering committee makes the decisions, and he bears no burden.

30

Always be
one step ahead

When everyone is focused on step N, you must be already working on step N+1 (and start thinking about step N+2).

At the project phase model, for example, it means that during the scoping phase, you should think about the project kick-off. When everyone is focused on the requirements, you should have the build phase in mind and so on.

At every level of the project, you should try

to anticipate what comes next.

This will help you ask good questions at the current step and identify all the points that need to be addressed before moving on.

It will also help you prepare for the next step, be sure that all prerequisites are met, and that the next team in line has everything they need to work.

One way I like to materialize that is by already having a draft to share when someone starts to talk about something that is far away in the planning.

31

Always offer solutions

There is no problem, only solutions.

Don't be a problem person; be a solution-giver.

Don't ever report a problem without presenting propositions to remediate it.

First, you don't have time during steering committees to brainstorm. Second, the rushed decision might not be the best one. Last and worst, it could generate noise around the project and, in the end, worsen the project.

As soon as something goes wrong, gather the team and imagine remediation scenarios. Detail each one of them, what could be done, what would be the impact on the scope, the budget, and planning. Rank them with the team, from the most preferred one to the least one. And present them to the steering committee.

The only thing a manager wants to hear is, "We are facing this situation. Here's what we can do. We can do this; it will require that and have this impact on the project. Or we can do that; it will require this and have that other impact. We strongly recommend the second option as it will allow us to do this."

32

Do not underestimate change management

Change management is clearly not the funniest part of the project.

Spending days explaining to people how they are going to use the product may not be that exciting. The fact is a product will be useless if users don't know how to operate it.

Mathematically, it's better to have a product that does 50% of the job that all the users know how to use than to have a perfect product that nobody knows how to use.

Change management is instrumental in a project. You can't improvise it.

It requires lots of planning and preparation, heavy documentation, and hours and hours of training for different kinds of populations.

From the very beginning of the project, during the scoping phase, you must carefully assess what it will take to train the users.

Think big. Don't limit the change to the strictly necessary, the basic quick training at the end of the project. You must wholly embrace the two main dimensions of change management:
- Communication and end-user engagement
- Skills development and training

On the communication side, plan to connect with the users as soon as possible and on a regular basis, in person and/or with a newsletter.

For the core part of the training, be ambitious. Your project deserves the best. Proper training requires a place, teachers, documentation, and a prototype.

Evaluate the necessary budget and validate it at the same moment as the project. Once again, it makes no sense to engage in a huge project with a tiny change in budget.

Later, change tasks cannot be postponed or deprioritized. Launch each planned change activity when they were expected.

The launch is also part of the change management stream. Should you go for a big kick-off or a quiet launch, be sure you have the budget and you have anticipated enough to ensure users are ready to welcome the product.

33

Risks can be opportunities

Fortune favors the bold.

A risk is an unsure event that would have an impact on your project.

This impact can be negative, but it can also be positive.

When you think about risks, you often only focus on dangerous events and situations that would cause a delay in your project or a budget increase.

But good things could also happen to your project.

For example, a key resource might be available sooner than expected. If you're not ready to react when the good news happens, if you did not anticipate that it could happen, you won't be ready, and you will be unable to take advantage of it.

From the very beginning of the project, every time you ask yourself what could go wrong, try to identify what could go better than expected.

During the project, monitor those opportunities closely; be careful about the risks.

34

Be agile or not, but deliver

Agile methodologies, scrum, in particular, are hugely popular now.

They are great. They have their advantages and limits.

You'll find plenty of books and articles talking about it.

The problem is that many project managers try to inject some agile practices into a non-agile project so they can claim they are agile. And by trying to have the best of both worlds, they end up with the worst.

Naming "user stories" in the chapters of your requirements and dividing your build into sprints does not make you agile.

Agile projects are built around small multi-disciplinary teams that build and validate a product iteratively. At any point, they could stop and release something, and the end-user would be able to begin to use it.

If you want to be truly agile, you must organize your project around small multidisciplinary teams and be sure that what is built is validated as the build goes on.

May I add that waterfall is a proven project methodology. Sometimes, you don't have to reinvent the wheel and go for the hype; just choose the approach everybody will understand and embrace.

35

Don't be indispensable

By positioning yourself on the critical path of every task, you will make your life a nightmare. Your days and nights will be filled with meetings, document reviews, e-mail processing, and validations.

You don't want that. You want to be able to take days off before the end of the project.

Your team doesn't want that.

Empower your team.

Each team member must have a scope of responsibility. Within this scope, they should feel trusted and entitled to make decisions and move things forward without having to refer to someone else.

Then, support your team. If they look for advice, let them know your office is open. If a choice they made appears to be bad, don't blame them. Help them to figure out how to correct the situation. Of course, if you see from afar that they're going to hit a wall, put a gentle hand on the steering wheel and guide them around the challenge.

Thus, all the members will be happy to work in your team, and you'll be able to enjoy your evenings and holidays.

36

Celebrate every achievement

A project can be a very long, monotonous funnel. Celebrating achievements, even small ones, will infuse energy and cultivate a positive mindset in the project team.

Celebrating does not necessarily mean organizing a big party with hundreds of invitees and an open bar. Keep that for the final ceremony.

Celebrating starts with a warm thank you and a tap on the shoulder to the couple of people who worked hard on a task or cracked a problem.

It can be organizing a breakfast with a part of the project team, during which people can present what they just delivered. It can be a lunch.

Of course, it can be having a drink after work.

Don't be shy about celebrating good news because people won't hesitate to pile in on your team when things go wrong.

37

Own the little boring tasks

You won't know much about your project if you fly miles above the battlefield.

Do not put yourself on a pedestal, disregarding all operational tasks to focus solely on high-level management matters. Embrace every small exercise; each one of them will give you a better grip on your project.

Need a small deck for tomorrow's committee? Don't ask and wait for someone to do it for you. Make your own selection of the best slides you can find on the shared folders.

A question on some figures discussed in a previous meeting? Get the file and get your head into it.

A team member needs a hand on a small task like gluing stamps or filling an Excel file? Take some time to help him.

For example, when I need figures, I don't ask for someone to prepare a slide for me. I ask to have access to the system that can provide me with them, and I dig by myself. I can see all the data available, the different variables and attributes. It takes more time, but if I need to refresh the data to adjust the report, I can do it in a second. And the next time I need data, I'll be able to find what I'm looking for very quickly.

Believe me, during a leadership committee, it's not hard to see who knows the data and who relies on someone else.

Managers who don't hesitate to dig into op-

erational and housekeeping tasks demon-
strate a much bigger control of their domain
than the ones who delegate everything.

38

The launch may be a project in itself

And one fine day, it's the launch.

But before the big celebration, there's a lot of work to do. And it better be carefully planned.

A launch is the convergence of many teams. Lots of small tasks will have to be performed by different people at a synchronized rhythm. It can quickly become a mess. You better take the time to prepare and plan it as precisely as possible.

Meet all the teams that are going to be involved. Go through all the activities they will have to perform. This is the same approach you followed during the framing phase to establish the project schedule. The difference is that you were at a week, maximum a day, granularity for the project plan, and for the launch, you should be at an hour, sometimes minute, granularity.

Specific governance could also be implemented with a dedicated meeting. It's the control tower that monitors what's happening and dispatches the various teams at the right time.

It would be a shame to have worked for months and missed the entire project due to a poor launch.

39

Dedicate a hyper-care team to support the launch

Even when carefully planned, a launch should be secured with a hyper-care system for a few weeks. A commando must be on the front.

Even if you delivered the product on time and on budget, if the launch is plagued with troubles and users are lost, that's what is going to be remembered of you and your project. The first impression counts, and the last one counts even more.

Precise processes must be carefully designed and implemented. People must be dedicated to being next to the end-users for the first days. Then, in the likely event of someone facing an issue or having a question, you must be crystal clear about who shall be called for help. The team on the other side of the line must have a decision/escalation tree that anticipates as many as possible plausible remediation solutions.

The support team must be over-trained, sharp, and master their stuff but also flexible enough to face any unexpected situation or question.

The more you prepare, the smoother the launch will be.

40

Transition to the day-to-day part of the organization

Remember the beginning of the book?

There are two worlds in companies: the projects, unique and timed, and the day-to-day business life, defined and repetitive.

What has been designed and built during a project must transition to the operational world, where it will be supported and sustained for a long time. This transition is your full responsibility.

Just like a bad launch, a bad transition to day-to-day operations can be a disaster for a project. And most insidious is that you won't see it instantly. Imagine a car manufacturer that launched a car but did a bad job at training the after-sale workshop network. The problem won't appear in the weeks following the launch, but the situation will appear months later.

During the project, you must identify who will support your product when launched. Contact these teams, present them with the project, and ask them what they need and when they need it.

Do what they ask.

Before the product launch, reach out to them and check that they are ready.

After the hyper-care period, when the time has come to handover, meet with the teams and verify for the last time that everything is under control.

After those last meetings, send an e-mail to every stakeholder and to every user of the product you may have met. Once again, share the day-to-day organization and processes and say farewell to everyone.

41

A good connection with leadership is key

A close connection with the sponsor is critical for the project's success; a good relationship with the executive committee will facilitate and smooth it.

Even the most extroverted leader won't say everything during a meeting. The only way to get to the bottom of topics and to truly know what they think is to see them one-on-one on a regular basis.

Depending on the individualities and agendas, you'll have to guess the best way and the right frequency to connect with them.

During your meetings, you'll have to show a deep interest in their challenges, stakes, and aspirations. What is discussed in these meetings should lead to concrete actions on your part. You'll have to prove that you care and that these meetings are valuable for these leaders. Otherwise, you'll lose their trust.

These exchanges will enable you to better lead your project teams, to better guide them, and to ensure that all perspectives have been considered.

42

Prepare every meeting

This rule is certainly relevant for the broader working world, but it is particularly pertinent in the context of project management.

Projects are high-paced entities where there's no place for waste of time. In that matter, you must be a role model. You owe it to yourself and to your team to arrive prepared and sharp for every meeting.

Do not tolerate any useless meetings.

Moreover, from a "management" perspective, preparing a meeting is not that hard:

The Simple Rules of Project Management

- Identify the owner of the meeting and warmly reach out to him.
- Check the meeting's purpose and goals (asking the question should at least ensure that it will be properly phrased for the meeting).
- Ask for the previous meeting' minutes (that's a killer).
- Identify if all key players are invited and present (we waste too much time waiting for people who haven't confirmed their attendance).
- Ask for the deck or pre-read (if there's none, you can request there will be one for the meeting).

It should take less than 5 minutes. The Return on Time Invested will be huge.

43

Organize a feedback session

Each project is an opportunity to learn and grow.

Once the project is completed and the product has been passed to the operational teams, gather everyone together one last time for a few hours.

The proposition is to identify what worked so that you can build on it for the next project and what didn't work so you can improve.

The Simple Rules of Project Management

It seems simple, but in practice, it's often complicated, especially the areas for improvement section.

People don't want to criticize their coworkers; they don't want to hurt anyone. The project manager must create a bubble of trust where everyone feels safe to share what can be improved, not with the aim of assigning blame but rather with the shared desire to progress together.

The first step is to brainstorm. Take any input, regardless of how it's given. Ensure every member can express themselves.

Then, group the various items by theme and discuss how they can be enhanced for the strengths or resolved for the weaknesses.

The deliverable of the meeting is a simple list of suggestions that each person is free to consider for their next ventures.

44

There is no glory for the project manager

At the end of the successful project, the person who gets the credit is the sponsor: the one who had the shoulders to support the project and approved the budget engagement. He will congratulate and thank the team and the project manager, but in the long term, he is the one who's going to leverage the product and reap the benefits.

Of course, as we have seen, in case of failure, the sponsor would not have been the blamed one.

But don't be demotivated.

First, a project is an amazing journey where you will learn a lot and meet amazing people. This is already a great compensation for all you will put in the project.

Second, I believe in karma. A good project manager who delivers and doesn't put himself before the project will be identified as a talent, someone the company can rely on. In the long term, good project managers are promoted.

Do your job, don't expect short-term specks, and wait for long-term rewards.

45

Always have a look at the bigger picture

Projects are often intense. The team is in a frenzy, taking on new tasks as soon as one is finished.

It's very easy to only see the pile of things to do and to forget the bigger purpose of what we do.

As a project manager, you are here to remind everyone why they are working hard and what they are working for.

It's not about building a plane; it's about allowing people to see their families; it's about allowing entrepreneurs to develop their businesses.

It's not about building a new distribution center; it's about people getting their gifts for Christmas.

It's not about developing a new diamond ring; it's about people celebrating their love.

And so on.

Keep the big picture in mind and, from time to time, make subtle allusions to it so that everyone keeps in mind how they are making a better place.

(This rule may not apply to the military or tobacco industry).

46

Don't be afraid to ask for help

Being a project may be a long road to travel. By design, you will be stretched outside your comfort zone.

Don't be surprised to feel lost. You'll have to learn new things. You will encounter new managerial situations.

The good news is there's a high probability that other people around you have already gone through similar experiences.

Don't be shy. Open up to others. Whatever their grade, they might have unexpected value to bring to you.

People often fear that sharing concerns with others may be seen as a sign of weakness. On the contrary, the most successful executives I've met had this quality: they ask people for their opinions.

It does not mean you have to do exactly what people say.

Collect advice, opinions, experiences, past mistakes, and so on. Mix that with your own beliefs and make your call.

Later, someone is going to come to you asking for your opinion on a challenge he faces, and you'll be in a position to reciprocate.

47

Stay positive and maintain a sense of humor

Life is too short to suffer at work.

As a manager, you're responsible for your team's work atmosphere.

Build a great team to work in. Be kind to everyone. Do not tolerate mean behavior. Give your attention to nice people, try to bring out the best in them, and don't waste your time on people who aren't worth it.

For your stakeholders, working on your

project should be a breath of fresh air regardless of what is happening in their affiliated departments.

Start to infuse this positive and enjoyable culture from the very beginning of the project. It won't be possible down the road when things will get hard.

Be serious, but don't take yourself too seriously.

Days will look shorter.

48

Great projects are great memories

When looking back on my career, I judge projects not on the quality of the deliverables but on the quality of the memories that remain.

Some projects are successful in the meaning that the specifications and requirements are met, but they do not carry any emotion.

In a great project, you feel something special. Even if tough at some points, all you remember are good memories. There's a team spirit, an emulation, a feeling of transcendence. There's a shared feeling that everyone is part of something special. When the project is completed and the team is disbanded, everyone will have heavy hearts.

Later, each one of the team members will recall that specific project with nostalgia. They will tell their story with passion, proud of what they were part of.

Enjoy the moment.

It's the journey that counts, not the destination. That is especially true for a project.

Cherish the team you're a part of, every unique individual. You're experiencing a one-of-a-kind harmony that may not happen again soon.

Printed in Great Britain
by Amazon